T0039391

CLOSE CALL

MARK LORING WHEELER

WESTBOW
PRESS®
A DIVISION OF THOMAS NELSON
& ZONDERVAN

Copyright © 2015 Mark Loring Wheeler.

All rights reserved. No part of this book may be used or reproduced by
any means, graphic, electronic, or mechanical, including photocopying,
recording, taping or by any information storage retrieval system
without the written permission of the author except in the case
of brief quotations embodied in critical articles and reviews.

WestBow Press books may be ordered through booksellers or by contacting:

WestBow Press
A Division of Thomas Nelson & Zondervan
1663 Liberty Drive
Bloomington, IN 47403
www.westbowpress.com
1 (866) 928-1240

Because of the dynamic nature of the Internet, any web addresses or
links contained in this book may have changed since publication and
may no longer be valid. The views expressed in this work are solely those
of the author and do not necessarily reflect the views of the publisher,
and the publisher hereby disclaims any responsibility for them.

Any people depicted in stock imagery provided by Thinkstock are models,
and such images are being used for illustrative purposes only.
Certain stock imagery © Thinkstock.

Cover Design by Megan Borthwell

ISBN: 978-1-5127-1952-9 (sc)
ISBN: 978-1-5127-1953-6 (e)

Library of Congress Control Number: 2015918669

Print information available on the last page.

WestBow Press rev. date: 11/20/2015

Unless otherwise indicated, Scripture is taken from the Revised Standard Version of the Bible, copyright 1952 [2nd edition, 1971] by the Division of Christian Education of the National Council of the Churches of Christ in the United States of America. Used by permission. All rights reserved.

Scripture marked TLB is taken from The Living Bible, copyright 1971. Used by permission of Tyndale House Publishers, Inc., Wheaton, Illinois 60189. All rights reserved.

Scripture marked NIV is taken from the HOLY BIBLE, NEW INTERNATIONAL VERSION. NIV. Copyright 1973, 1978, 1984 by International Bible Society. Used by permission of Zondervan. All rights reserved.

Scripture marked NASB is taken from the New American Standard Bible, copyright 1960, 1962, 1963, 1968, 1971, 1972 by the Lockman Foundation, La Habra, California. Used by permission.

Scripture marked NLT is taken from The Holy Bible, New Living Translation, copyright 1996, 2004, 2007 by Tyndale House Foundation. Used by permission of Tyndale House Publishers, Inc., Carol Stream, Illinois 60188. All rights reserved.

Scripture marked ESV is taken from The Holy Bible, English Standard Version (ESV), copyright 2001 by Crossway, a publishing ministry of Good News Publishers. Used by permission. All rights reserved.

CONTENTS

With profound gratitude to my wife and best friend, Patty, who hung in there through it all—through the emergency notifications, the endless, lonely nights of wondering, and the periods when I wasn't very loveable. I thank my daughters, Becky and Megan, who each in her own way endured the collateral effects of being a CK (cop's kid) and a PK (pastor's kid) but kept God first and still made me feel like a superhero. You have blessed me immeasurably, and for that I am eternally grateful.

PREFACE

"I knew you before I formed you in your mother's womb. Before you were born I set you apart and appointed you as my prophet to the nations."

"O sovereign Lord," I said, "I can't speak for you! I'm too young!"

The Lord replied, "Don't say, 'I'm too young', for you must go wherever I send you and say whatever I tell you. And don't be afraid of the people, for I will be with you and will protect you. I, the Lord, have spoken!" Then the Lord reached out and touched my mouth and said, "Look, I have put my words in your mouth!"

—Jeremiah 1:5–9 (NLT)

A few years ago, Patty and I spent an incredible evening with a very dear couple we had drawn close to while working together to restore a local pastor and his ministry. While we had known them for years through church, we had never really taken the time to socialize. It had been pretty much a casual acquaintance. This particular evening was all about getting to know each other better.

After dinner at a local Japanese steakhouse, we returned to their house to kick back and relax. It wasn't long before they began sharing openly about their experiences growing up, how they met, and of course, about their walk with God. It was really cool listening to them as they reminisced and reflected. Both were US Army veterans. In fact, they'd met while serving. She was a former personnel admin specialist. He was a retired helicopter pilot who had flown combat missions in Southeast Asia and the Middle East. Listening to them was more than captivating. Patty and I were absolutely enthralled. Then it was our turn. "Tell us about you," they said. I remember responding almost immediately with, "Are you sure? Our story reads more like a novel than a real-life biography. You won't believe it." And I really meant it. Of course they ignored my hesitation and responded, "Come on, tell us!" Well, I think that night was the first time we had told the whole story—the unedited version of the Wheeler saga. For some reason, this time just seemed like the right time. Why? I'm not really sure. I think it was because we had made a connection we had never made before, and we trusted them. When we were through telling our story, they just looked at us in amazement and said something to the effect of "Wow! You guys have a real story! We had no idea!"

It wasn't until later that night that the reality of all we had been through really hit me. We had endured trial after trial, close call after close call. But why?

When we backed out of their driveway later that night, Patty looked at me with a look I had seen only a few times in all the years we had been together and said, "Mark, you *need* to write a book!" Of course, I had joked many times over the years about writing a book—in fact, several books. I had even proposed catchy titles for each one of them, titles like *Riding Solo on a Two-Man Patrol, All for the Wrong Reasons,* and *Four Walls and a Utility Bill.* But until this particular night, they were never really a serious consideration. Writing a book had been nothing more than a pipe dream. In my mind, writing was reserved for just about everyone but me. Write a book? Are you serious? I could hardly come up with enough words to complete my first essay in English Comp 101, let alone write a book. One after another, all of the "yeah, buts" rolled off my tongue as we drove home. It was obvious that the pipe dream mentality was deeply rooted in my psyche. All of the reasons—or should I say excuses—for why I could never write a book kept playing over and over in my head. Yet I couldn't deny what had happened. God had given me an appointment and an assignment. He had given me revelation and confirmation. He had spoken a powerful and significant word into my heart. He had given me the "why" and the "want to." All I had to do was act on it.

Well, I wish I could say I bounced out of bed that very next morning and with a feverish exuberance began knocking out chapter after inspired chapter. But that was not the case. It would be several years—eight, to be exact—before I mustered enough gumption to write the first sentence. It wasn't until after I was diagnosed with colon cancer and had undergone nine major surgeries that the "why" and the "want to" became real enough to deliver me from what seemed like a terminal case of procrastination. Now, don't get me wrong. It wasn't like I had been struck suddenly with some newfound sense of mortality, nor was my change in attitude a knee-jerk reaction to a recent near-death experience. It wasn't like that at all. My attitude change was, in fact, a heart change—a heart change that had renewed my sense of purpose and belief. A purpose and belief that said, "You are set apart! You can do this! You are called to do this!" In other words, the "why" God had given me had breathed life into my "want to" and had overcome my fears. It was time to go where He had told me to go and tell the story that He had told me to tell. After all, as with Jeremiah, He had put His words in my mouth.

ACKNOWLEDGMENTS

Almighty God,

my Lord, my Savior, my Redeemer, my all in all, thank
You for seeing in me what I am unable to see in myself.

Patty,

my wife, thank you for your love, continuous
prayer, and constant encouragement

Megan Loring Borthwell,

my daughter, thank you for your watchful eye
and creative insight, without which the cover of
this book would not be as awesome as it is.

Brian Andre Borthwell,

my son-in-law, thank you for helping an old
school dinosaur make sense of today's technology.
Your technical expertise was invaluable.

My friends,

thank you for your love, sincere interest, and incredible support. It kept me focused and motivated. It gave me a reason to finish.

McKenzie Grogan,

my publishing consultant, thank you for listening. Your sweet spirit blessed and encouraged me.

Dr. Travis Crudup, Dr. Robert M. Goldstein, Dr. Lori Gordon, and Dr. Louis Strock,

my surgeons, thank you for allowing God to work through you. Thank you for caring!

INTRODUCTION

As I sit here gazing out my office window, which overlooks my beautiful front yard, I find myself wrestling with a gamut of emotions—excitement because I've finally written the book that's been in my heart for years; a sense of achievement because procrastination and inertia no longer have a grip on me, at least for the time being; intimidation because of the incredible implications of this work; humility for having been entrusted with such an awesome assignment; and gratitude for a loving, gracious, and merciful God, who, before time began, saw something in me that it would take almost a lifetime for me to see in myself.

Okay. Now that we're done with the mushy, reflective stuff, let's get down to brass tacks, as my mother used to say, and lay some groundwork.

This book is not intended or presented as a literary masterpiece, nor will it be a likely candidate for the *New York Times* best seller list, although that would be nice. It will not have the fit and finish of a refined work. It won't be laden with complex concepts and complicated theology. It won't be lengthy and tedious. And I promise it won't lull you to sleep. It will be concise and to the point because that is what I was taught in school. It will be honest, sincere, and accurate, at least to the best of my recollection. It will be from my heart.

Hopefully, in the few short chapters that follow, you will come to the realization that it took me almost a lifetime to achieve: the events in our lives are not random, isolated occurrences but rather divinely orchestrated, providential experiences that prepare us for a much greater purpose—that is, if we let them. For me it was a series of life-threatening experiences—twelve of them, to be exact.

PROLOGUE

He regulates the Universe by the power
of His command.

—Hebrews 1:2–3 (TLB)

Have you ever had a harrowing or nerve-wracking experience and, when it was all over, thought to yourself, *Whew! That was a close call!* Sure you have. We all have. Close calls happen every day to people just like you and me. But think for a moment. Have you ever wondered why? Have you chosen to view these events as divine orchestrations over time, or have you simply dismissed them as random, isolated occurrences? Did you think to thank God when you were eventually spared, or when a disaster threatening the safety or welfare of others was averted? I mean *really* thank God? Did you say with conviction in your heart, "Thanks be to God!" or merely blurt out with a sigh of relief, "Thank God that's over!"? Or were you so wrapped up in the excitement of the event that you never even considered God's involvement? For many of us, the latter hits the nail on the head. We narrowly escape, breathe a sigh of relief, consider ourselves lucky, and press on. Rarely, if ever, do we view the close calls in our lives as divinely orchestrated, providential experiences with specific purposes and eternal implications.

Consider this exchange between God and the prophet Jeremiah.

> "Go down to the potter's shop and I will speak to you there." So I did as he told me and found the potter working at his wheel. But the jar he was making did not turn out as he had hoped, so he crushed it into a lump of clay again and started over. (Jeremiah 18:2-4 NLT)

As the potter would mold or shape a clay pot on the potter's wheel, defects would often appear. As the wheel turned, the potter had power over the clay to either allow the defects or reshape the pot. Likewise, God has the power to reshape us, just like Judah, to conform to His purposes. As we acknowledge Him and turn from our old ways, He begins reshaping us into the valuable vessels He intended us to be. He prepares us.

Journey with me as I share a series of life-threatening events that occurred over a period of almost forty years—events that had a profound impact on my life and eventually molded me into the man I am today. See how God reshaped me into the vessel He had hoped for, the person I was *set apart* and *appointed* to be.

CHAPTER 1

TWELVE STONES

---✦---

When the whole nation had finished crossing the Jordan, the Lord said to Joshua, "Choose twelve men from among the people, one from each tribe, and tell them to take up twelve stones from the middle of the Jordan from right where the priests stood and to carry them over with you and put them down at the place where you stay tonight."

—Joshua 4:1–3 (NIV)

As the people of Israel safely crossed the Jordan River into the Promised Land, God directed them to build a monument. While this may seem like a curious directive, God did not want His people to jump headlong into their new lives, their new land, and their new assignments unprepared and unsupported. It was imperative that they focused on Him and remembered who was guiding them, protecting them, and caring for them.

> So Joshua called together the twelve men
> he had appointed from the Israelites, one
> from each tribe, and said to them, "Go
> over before the ark of the Lord your God
> into the middle of the Jordan. Each of
> you is to take up a stone on his shoulder,
> according to the number of the tribes of
> the Israelites, to serve as a sign among
> you. In the future, when your children
> ask you, 'What do these stones mean?'
> Tell them that the flow of the Jordan was
> cut off before the ark of the covenant of
> the Lord. When it crossed the Jordan, the
> waters of the Jordan were cut off. These
> stones are to be a memorial to the people
> of Israel forever." (Joshua 4:4-7 NIV)

Joshua and the nation of Israel erected a monument—a
memorial to commemorate the end of their wandering
and the beginning of their new lives. While monuments
are usually erected to commemorate significant historical
events or acknowledge heroic deeds, individual lives
have special monuments also. They can be special events,
answered prayers, or even miracles. For me it was a series
of life-threatening events. God used them to shape me
and equip me. Each *close call* was a stone—a stone with
which to build a monument. This monument is meant to
remind me who I am and who I am called to be. It is a
monument to remind me who is guiding me, protecting
me, and caring for me. This monument would teach me
and remind me that the close call events in my life are

not just random, unrelated, insignificant occurrences but rather truly significant, divinely orchestrated, providential acts of love designed to shape me, prepare me, and make me more like Him.

The monument of twelve stones was to be a constant reminder of the moment when the Israelites crossed the Jordan River on dry ground. Their children would see the stones, hear the story, and grow in their knowledge of God.

It has been my prayer from the beginning that through this book my children, their children, and all those willing would see the stones, hear the story, and ultimately grow in their knowledge of God.

CHAPTER 2

HOW IT ALL BEGAN

Jesus replied, "You do not realize now
what I am doing, but later you will
understand."

—John 13:7 (NIV)

I looked up, and all I could see was a big rig bearing down
on me from the left. I stomped on the accelerator, my
pride and joy hooked, and with a roar any gearhead would
be proud of, we were off. Well, almost. In the blink of
an eye a massive shadow appeared to my right, and the
deafening sound of an air horn filled the air. I turned the
steering wheel hard to the left, and in an instant it seemed
like everything was happening in slow motion. The initial
impact slid me across my freshly reconditioned leather seat
and against the passenger door. A second impact slid me
back across the seat. My door swung open, and out I went,
headfirst, narrowly missing a telephone pole and support
cable. The next thing I knew, I was lying facedown in a
grassy field. I lay there for a minute or two, then stood

up, looked back toward the intersection, and thought to myself, *Man, that was close. I'm glad I missed that telephone pole.* Right then, a man in a gray work shirt ran over to me in a panic and said, "Son, are you okay?"

It was June 26, 1972. I had completed my freshmen year at Clemson University and was about to start my first day of summer work. I was really excited because I was returning to work at a day camp where I had worked since I was a sophomore in high school. I had worked my way up from preschool counselor to waterfront director. Talk about a dream summer job. Anyway, I awoke early that day because I wanted to make sure I got to the pool in time to set up, brief my assistant, and test the water before the kids arrived for morning lessons. I showered, made my lunch, packed my gym bag full of the usual lifeguard stuff, and out the door I went. I was pumped. I was also excited about showing off my pride and joy—a Milano Maroon 1966 Chevy Impala with a bored-out engine, a bunch of bolt-on performance parts, chrome wheels, a black vinyl top, and an exhaust system that would rattle your windows.

She had been sitting out all night and was covered in dew. While this was not an uncommon phenomenon for cool summer mornings, it wasn't exactly one I wanted to mess with on this particular morning, especially since I was trying to get an early start. I quickly wiped the dew from the windows, fired the "Mark-mobile" up, and away we went. Now, if you are not familiar with older carbureted car engines, they are equipped with an auto choke. When the engine is cold, the choke engages and causes the engine to idle faster. When the engine warms up, the choke disengages and the engine then idles at normal speed. Occasionally, the choke will stick and you have to "kick it down" by revving the engine. Now, for those of you familiar with muscle cars, you probably know some of them have a tendency to be rather cold natured. Well, guess what? The Mark-mobile was no exception. When I got to the intersection about two blocks from my house, the tachometer was still reading about 1,500 rpms, and I could still feel the engine pulling against the brakes. Consequently, I had to brake harder than normal in order to stop at the intersection. The abrupt stop caused my lunch to slide off the seat and onto the floorboard. Like a dummy, I reached down and grabbed it. But by the time I sat up, the Mark-mobile had inched out into the intersection and directly into the path of an approaching eighteen-wheeler. Not having time to put it in reverse, I floored it, hoping to get through the intersection and out of its way. What I didn't anticipate was the approach of another eighteen-wheeler coming from the opposite direction. And, well, you know the rest. My pride and joy was pretty much demolished, except for the wheels and a pair of 8-ohm speakers. On the bright side, however, except for a mild case of shock, I survived relatively unscathed. That's right. I had survived a broadside collision with a fully loaded eighteen-wheeler traveling at 50 mph and a subsequent ejection. No one, including the drivers of the eighteen-wheelers or the responding emergency personnel, could believe I was alive. And frankly, neither could I.

Now you're probably thinking that surely this is where he fell to his knees, dedicated his life to the Lord, and embedded himself in a youth group or young-adult Bible class. *Au contraire!* Not even close. In fact, nothing like that ever crossed my mind. Don't get me wrong. I believed in God. I even believed in Jesus and the Holy Spirit. I had been raised in the church. I received communion at least once a month, served as an acolyte (altar boy), and sang in the choir. I could recite the Lord's Prayer, the Nicene Creed, the Apostles' Creed, the Twenty-third Psalm, Psalm 100, and more. In fact, I had attended just about every church in the city of Clemson during my freshmen year. And that was without parental prodding. But was God at the center of my everyday life? No. Sadly, He wasn't.

So yes, this is where the remolding process began. I just wouldn't realize it until many years later.

Close Call #1

Case Notes:

The following passage would eventually prove to be a prophetic promise that characterized the next forty-plus years of my life.

> Blessed be God the Father of our Lord and Savior Jesus Christ, who according to His great mercy has caused us to be born again to a living hope through the resurrection of Jesus Christ from the dead, to obtain

an inheritance which is imperishable and undefiled and will not fade away, reserved in heaven for you, who are *protected* by the power of God through faith for a salvation ready to be revealed in the last time. In this you greatly rejoice, even though now for a little while, if necessary, you have been *distressed by various trials*, so that the proof of your faith, being more precious than gold which is perishable, even though *tested* by fire, may be found to result in praise and glory and honor at the revelation of Jesus Christ, and though you have not seen Him, you love Him, and though you do not see Him now, but *believe in Him*, you greatly rejoice with joy inexpressible and full of glory obtaining as the outcome of your faith the salvation of your soul. (1 Peter 1:1–9 TLB; emphasis mine)

CHAPTER 3

Two Down

But in that coming day no weapon turned
against you will succeed. You will silence
every voice raised up to accuse you.

-Isaiah 54:17 (NLT)

Wow! I've heard of writer's block, but I never thought
it would manifest this quickly and be this complete. I'm
only on the third chapter of my first book, and I'm already
dead in the water. Why I am I struggling like this? Why
am I having trouble finding the words to chronicle the
most significant and prolific challenge of my life? Why
am I shutting down? Where are the words?

For the sake of candor and transparency, I started this
chapter by sharing with you my thoughts in the days
before actually writing it.

Here's why. Follow closely.

Francesco Vincent Serpico is most notably known as the first police officer in the history of the New York City Police Department (NYPD) to report and openly testify to widespread, systematic corruption within police ranks. He is credited with contributing to an April 25, 1970, *New York Times* front-page story on police corruption, which eventually led to the formation of the Knapp Commission, an independent investigative panel.

On February 3, 1971, Serpico, a twelve-year veteran, was shot once in the face during an attempted drug arrest at an apartment building in Brooklyn. The bullet struck him just below his eye and lodged at the top of his jaw. He was able to fire back once before falling helplessly to the hallway floor. Even though he was bleeding profusely, fellow officers refused to call for help or advise headquarters that an officer had been shot. Fortunately, an elderly resident in the adjacent apartment called for help while a stranger rendered aid. Ironically, a police patrol unit arrived on the scene first. Not realizing who he was, the responding officers transported Serpico to the hospital.

The bullet that struck Serpico severed an auditory nerve, leaving him deaf in one ear and suffering chronic pain due to bullet fragments still lodged in his brain. Serpico recovered, however, and eventually testified openly before the Knapp Commission. His testimony resulted in the largest shake-up in department history and the formation of the Commission to Combat Police Corruption, an independent board that still operates today.

Serpico's shooting, although highly questionable, was never formally investigated. It is widely believed Serpico was set up by fellow officers and led unknowingly to that particular apartment to be executed.

Frank Serpico retired on June 15, 1972, one month after receiving the New York City Police Department's highest award, the Medal of Honor. The medal was not presented in a formal ceremony. It was simply handed to him.

Serpico became famous after the release of the 1973 movie *Serpico*, which starred Al Pacino. He still lives in semiseclusion.

Now you are probably wondering what all of this Serpico stuff has to do with my writer's block. Here's the connection.

On October 24, 1974, at the ripe old age of twenty-one, I was commissioned a deputy sheriff. It was an incredibly auspicious occasion. It was the realization of a childhood dream. Unfortunately, by the time I had served three years and had barely reached the age of twenty-four, I had weathered several Internal Affairs investigations and testified before two investigative grand juries regarding widespread corruption within the department. I had reported numerous acts of corruption and misconduct to my superiors only to find out that they too were deeply involved. I had testified against my partner in open court and watched while he was sentenced to five years in prison and taken into custody as his wife looked on. I had endured the snub of fellow officers and experienced the distrust of the Solicitor's Office (district attorney) and the State Law Enforcement Division. I had been named in an intelligence report as one of three targets on a bona fide hit list. I had relocated my wife due to growing concerns for her safety, partnered with a former Navy Seal with explosive ordinance (bomb disposal) expertise, and delivered my first daughter under a fictitious name. I had been jokingly nicknamed Serpico.

Then it got worse. In December 1976, an article appeared in the morning edition of the local newspaper naming deputies who would not be retained by the newly elected sheriff due to substandard job performance. My name was on the list. To make matters even worse, shortly after being shown the article at roll call that morning, I received an urgent call from Patty. She had been handed a copy of the article at work and was devastated. I can't even begin to describe the feeling in the pit of my stomach. It was beyond nauseated. It was beyond excruciating. Never before had I experienced such disgrace, such dishonor. I felt filthy. I had let Patty and my little girl down. I had failed to insulate them and protect them. My ability to provide for them was in serious jeopardy. It was a sentence they didn't deserve.

A few days later, I asked my lieutenant (the honest one, that is), why the sheriff-elect wouldn't keep me. He told me that he had spoken to the sheriff-elect on my behalf, and although he liked me and acknowledged my exemplary record, he wasn't willing to bear the political heat of retaining me.

In acknowledgment of my exemplary record, I was eventually given the opportunity to resign rather than be dismissed. Two weeks later, on my last day as a deputy sheriff, I was formally recognized for outstanding performance and presented with a plaque. The plaque had my retired badge mounted on it with an inscription below it that read, "From Your Friends—Bravo Shift." My dismissal for substandard performance reported by the local newspaper was never retracted.

For a young man raised primarily in a small township in rural New Jersey by a conservative southern family, this was more than just a bad employment experience. This was worse than a bad dream. This was a bona fide nightmare, a disgrace that would haunt me and my family for years to come.

On April 17, 1977, after a brief stint selling cars at a local Chevrolet dealership, I enlisted in the United States Air Force with a guaranteed assignment in the security police field. I enlisted with five primary goals: (1) to provide a stable source of income for my family; (2) exonerate myself; (3) regain my family's trust and admiration; (4) restore my sense of self-worth; and (5) complete my education.

I completed basic training with honors and eventually graduated first in my class at the US Air Force Security Police Academy. I was presented the Distinguished Honor Graduate Award and recognized as the first trainee in the history of the academy to graduate with a perfect score. From there I went on to Air Base Ground Defense

(Combat) Training, again graduating with distinction. I was eventually assigned to the 380th Security Police Squadron (SAC), Plattsburgh Air Force, Plattsburgh, NY.

During my roughly six years at Plattsburgh AFB, I attained top secret security clearance, held several supervisory positions, and rose to the rank of staff sergeant. I completed undergraduate degrees in criminal justice, police science, and sociology/criminology and began work on my master's in systems management.

Now, for the sake of the brevity, which I promised in my preface (if you skipped the preface, introduction, and prologue, now would be a good time to go back and read them), I am going to fast-forward to February 1982.

On 3 February 1983 (that's a military date), I was honorably discharged from the United States Air Force. Upon separation I was awarded the Air Force Commendation Medal for meritorious service.

Shortly after returning to our home of record, Patty landed an assistant manager's position at one of the largest banks in town. Roughly thirty days later, I was rehired as a deputy by the sheriff who, roughly six years earlier, refused to take a chance on me. In addition, I was given pay differentials for previous experience and education. I was recommissioned after completing a two-week legal refresher course at the State Criminal Justice Academy.

During my law enforcement career, I held positions in Uniform Patrol, Special Operations (Vice and Narcotics), and Economic (White Collar) Crime. I also served as an instructor in officer survival and was a member of the dive team.

Close Call #2

Case Notes:

To this day, I am the sole survivor of that hit list. The other individuals named (one of which was a former deputy sheriff) were found brutally murdered not long after the list came to light.

CHAPTER 4

MYSTERY DRIVER

His eye is on the sparrow and I know He
watches over me.

—Civilla D. Martin

Have you ever seen or sensed something developing in
front of you, but because your mind was focused on
something else, you didn't pay much attention to it?
Well, maybe not. But that's what happened to me on this
particular night.

I had just picked up my partner, and we were headed
to roll call. Our regular car had been in the shop for
several days, so we were still driving a spare. It was a
muggy night, and the A/C in the spare wasn't working
very well. We were both sweating bullets. My partner
had played golf all day, and I could tell that he was really
tired. He wasn't saying much. He was just sitting there in
the passenger's seat with his head back and his eyes half-
closed. We had recently rotated to third shift from first so

we were both dragging a little. Third shift was midnight to 8:00 a.m., and roll call was at 11:30 p.m.

It was about eleven fifteen in the evening, and we were still at least fifteen minutes from headquarters. As I was driving, I vaguely remember a car approaching in the northbound lane rather slowly and then turn left as if to cross through the median. Admittedly, I wasn't paying very close attention. I just assumed it was doing a U-turn, which was perfectly legal in that particular spot. It was rather hilly where we were, so I lost sight of it temporarily as we went downhill. As we topped the next hill, I couldn't believe my eyes. There it was smack-dab in the middle of the highway. Dead in front of us, broadside across both lanes, sat a full-size, four-door sedan. Can you picture it? We're less than one hundred feet away and heading downhill at sixty miles per hour. I hit my high beams and laid on the horn. Our lights lit up the car's entire passenger compartment. I could see a lone, middle-aged female just sitting there staring into our headlights. She looked mesmerized. Frozen. I remember thinking, *I can't hit this woman. If I hit her, she'll never survive.* Right then, my academy training kicked in. I slammed on the brakes, turned hard to the right, and put us into a controlled slide. I gunned it and turned back hard to the left, hoping to swing the rear end back around. I thought if I could execute a modified bootleg maneuver we could avoid hitting her all together. Before the rear end came completely around, the right front tire dipped into a drainage culvert on the shoulder of the road, burying the nose of our car. The rear end immediately went vertical. From that point on everything seemed like it was moving in slow motion. I remember thinking, *Wow, this is a familiar sensation.* As the rear end came completely over, we inverted and started to roll. My partner was thrown into the air like a 220-pound rag doll. As he flew over me, his knee hit me in the face and snapped my head back into the headrest. I was dazed but still conscious. As we continued to roll, he fell back into me from the backseat, smashing my face into the steering wheel. We rolled several more times and eventually came to rest, right side up, on a hill overlooking the highway. It was surreal. I felt like I had gone fifteen rounds with Joe Frazier. The roof of the car was completely compressed and was now level with the hood and trunk lid. We were jammed in like a pair of sardines in a can. At first I couldn't get my seatbelt to release. I looked down to see what was wrong, and I couldn't believe what I saw. My pistol had been ripped from my holster and was wedged in the mangled seat. The force of my weight pulling against it as we rolled had torn the leather. That's right! My patent leather holster was torn. I mean, ripped in half! We crawled out through the passenger side and scrambled up the hill and away from the car. I looked back, and the passenger door was completely gone. The emergency lights were gone. The engine throttle was stuck, so the wheels were still spinning and that high-performance engine was screaming. Smoke and the smell of gas filled the air. I hollered to my partner to call for help, but he was incoherent and kept yelling that his foot was gone. I could see that his foot was okay, but I could tell that he was going into shock. My face and hands were covered in blood. I looked frantically for one of the portable radios, but I couldn't find one. I started to lose consciousness and fell to the ground. While I was lying there, a lone, middle-aged woman ran toward me hollering, "I'm so sorry! I'm so sorry! I didn't mean to pull in front of you." I remember smelling the odor of alcohol. Then suddenly she disappeared. I fought to stay awake. I could hear the yelp of sirens coming from every direction and see blue lights everywhere. They were the most welcome sights and sounds I had ever experienced. Before I knew it, I was in an EMS unit with paramedics hovering over me. I could hear them talking to the ER doctor on the radio. I could hear them transmitting my vitals as they wiped blood from my face. I remember thinking, *My vitals aren't good. I really don't want to hear all of this.* I was delirious. I remember asking, "Where's my partner? Is he okay?" I don't remember ever getting an answer.

We spent the next three days in the hospital for observation. Miraculously, other than considerable bruising, neither one of us had any major injuries. I wound up with a broken nose, and my partner had some minor burns and a few abrasions.

The morning after the accident a middle-aged man came to see us. He walked in the room, introduced himself as the driver of the other car, and said, "I'm so glad you guys are okay. I didn't mean to pull in front of you, but you guys were really moving!" My partner and I just looked at each other. We were stunned! I said, "Sir, you weren't driving that car. It was a woman driving. What's going on?" He said, "No, I was driving. You must be confused."

I was infuriated! I said, "Sir, you need to leave the room right now!" He hesitated for a moment and left.

A short time later, a sergeant from the Highway Patrol stopped by to check on us and let us know that his team had completed their investigation. He advised us that the length of our skid marks indicated we were exceeding the speed limit, but he also commented that whoever was driving the patrol car did an incredible job of avoiding the other car. I told the sergeant that I was driving, that I wasn't speeding, and that the driver of the other car was a woman and not the man who had just visited. I told him that she had run up the hill to check on us after we crashed and that I could smell alcohol on her breath. He just dismissed my comments and played it off like I was delirious or suffering from sort of post-traumatic shock. By this time I was really upset, and so was my partner. We were completely lucid, and everybody was treating us like we were nuts. This whole thing smelled like a major cover-up.

Just to give you a little background information, my partner was an ex-Navy Seal and the sheriff's department's resident bomb technician. He had been assigned to me for personal protection shortly after the hit list came to light. He was a veteran deputy and could smell a rat in the woodpile as well as anyone. He was convinced that someone influential was covering for the true driver of the car. I agreed.

Close Call #3

Case Notes:

About two days after we were discharged from the hospital, we were ordered by the sheriff to "Drop it!" I was told, in no uncertain terms, I should be thankful that I hadn't been charged with reckless driving and that both my partner and I were lucky to still have jobs.

To this very day the identity of the other driver remains a mystery.

CHAPTER 5

Bridge Out

For He will command His angels concerning you to guard you in all your ways; they will lift you up in their hands, so that you will not strike your foot against a stone.

—Psalm 91:11–12 (NIV)

It's been raining for almost six weeks. The creeks and rivers are overflowing, and just about everything is underwater. It's like one big pond around here. Frankly, I'm sick and tired of being soaked. My throat is sore, my head hurts, and my voice is about gone. My car windows stay fogged up all the time, and I can hardly see where I'm going. This is not fun!

Those were my thoughts just minutes before I experienced one of the most life-threatening and heart-wrenching events of my life.

It was early spring, and we were getting drenched by torrential rains. Patty and I were living in our mobile home at the time, and you could hear just about every raindrop that fell. In a gentle rain it was great—in fact, downright soothing. But a heavy rain was definitely another story. It sounded like were living in a tin can. Well, we were, but it wasn't supposed to sound like one.

Anyway, I think it was a Saturday night. Patty was in bed watching the *Tonight Show* with Johnny Carson, and little Becky was asleep in the front bedroom. Bless her heart; she could sleep through a nuclear blast. I donned my full-length rain slicker, covered my wool felt campaign hat (we wore hats like drill sergeants back then), grabbed a towel, and away I went.

Conditions were exceptionally poor. I signed on directly from the trailer and headed north. Tornadoes were dropping all over the county, so we were all assigned spotter duty. That's right! We actually went out looking for those things. And that was before Doppler radar. Not a fun assignment.

Anyway, I had completed my first spotter run up north and was headed back. Just to change things up a little and break the monotony, I decided to head a little further south than normal into the adjoining patrol beat. My plan was to turn west, cross over the river, and circle back along the county line into my regular beat. It was raining steadily, and visibility was poor. As I turned west, I noticed a station wagon about four or five car lengths ahead of me. I remember thinking, *What in the world is anybody doing out at this time of night in this kind of weather?* The road was covered with standing water, so I was keeping my distance. As the station wagon rounded the curve in front of us, I temporarily lost sight of it. There were no street lights on this particular stretch of road, and it was unusually dark. As I rounded the curve, I was expecting to see taillights. There were none. No taillights and no headlights. No lights at all. The station wagon was gone. I mean gone, gone! Vanished! And there were no turnoffs, nowhere for it to have gone. I instinctively slammed on the breaks. My car started to slide. I corrected and held on, just praying it would stop before I slid off the road or into a tree. Miraculously, the tires grabbed in just a few seconds, and I came to a stop dead in the middle of the road. I hit my high beams, but there was nothing there. The road was gone. Completely gone. There was nothing but a black hole. I could hear the sound of rushing water even though my windows were closed. I activated my emergency lights and spot, stepped out, and rushed to the front of my car. I was not prepared for what I saw. It was like a sink hole awash with white water rapids. The drop-off was just inches from my front bumper. I looked down, and I could see the station wagon's headlights flickering beneath the water. I was sickened by the thought of someone being trapped inside. The station wagon rolled as the current hit it, and it sank deeper into the river. I took my shoes and gun belt off and slid down the embankment. I wanted so badly to dive in, but the current was just too strong. I looked for a place to wade in, but it was just too slippery. There was nothing to hold on to. I felt helpless. All I could do was watch as the station wagon disappeared from sight. I crawled back up the embankment and radioed for help. By this time there were cars stopped on both sides of the river. Miraculously, my lights had warned them in time.

It wasn't until daylight that we were able to string enough cable from one side of the river to the other to secure diver safety lines. It took two truck wreckers, one on each side, and an army of volunteers to do it.

Around ten o'clock the current slowed and the river receded enough for the divers to go in. It wasn't long after that the station wagon was being pulled from the river.

What followed on this Sunday morning would stay with me forever. As the rear of the station wagon broke the surface of the water, a tiny body floated from an open window. The body was that of a three-year-old little girl. Her mother's body was later recovered from the vehicle.

Close Call #4

Case Notes:

To be honest, I really don't know what to say or where to go from here. God spared me, not that little girl or her mother. Had I not lost sight of those taillights, had they not driven into that watery abyss first, I would not be writing this account. For that I have no words of my own. I can only offer what was spoken to the prophet Isaiah and affirmed by the apostle Paul.

"'My thoughts are nothing like your thoughts,' says the Lord. 'And my ways are far beyond anything you could imagine. For just as the heavens are higher than the earth, so my ways are higher than your ways and my thoughts higher than your thoughts'" (Isaiah 55:8–9 NLT).

"And we know that God causes everything to work together for the good of those who love God and are called according to his purpose for them" (Romans 8:28 NLT).

CHAPTER 6

SHOOT/DON'T SHOOT

Though a thousand fall at your side,
though ten thousand are dying around
you, these evils will not touch you.

—Psalm 91:7 (NLT)

Have you ever been forced to make a split second life-or-death decision? Have you ever had to decide whether or not to take someone else's life in order to save your own? I certainly hope not. But unfortunately, this is a decision I would be forced to make on this particular summer afternoon.

It was about an hour into the shift when my sergeant gave me what I thought was a relatively benign assignment.

I was to make a courtesy check of an apartment residence maintained by a local attorney. According to the information I was provided, the attorney requested the check because he was concerned that his estranged wife might try to break in and steal his 9mm Luger pistol. He indicated in his request that his soon-to-be ex-wife had already made several threats and he was afraid that she would do something drastic. I was given an address and a description of the estranged wife's vehicle.

Shortly after meeting with my sergeant, I drove to the apartment to conduct my first check. As soon as I pulled into the main driveway of the complex, I noticed a vehicle matching the description of the wife's car coming toward me from the general vicinity of the attorney's apartment. As it got closer, I slowed to a near stop and pulled toward the curb. Suddenly, the vehicle accelerated, turned sharply into my lane, and rammed me. I was stunned. I couldn't believe what had just happened. I radioed for assistance and jumped out, using my car door for cover. I couldn't see the driver clearly. It was a sunny afternoon, and the glare from the windshield was obscuring my vision. I hesitated for a second, stood up, and walked slowly toward the car. Just before I reached the front bumper, the driver of the car sat straight up and leveled a pistol directly at me. I couldn't believe it! It was beyond surreal. She had gotten the drop on me and was going to fire right through the windshield. I remember saying to myself, *Mark, this is not a shoot/don't shoot simulation. This is the real deal.* Then tunnel vision kicked in, and I felt like I was in a movie. She pushed the pistol forward and pulled the trigger. Nothing happened. I drew my weapon and instinctively dropped to one knee. She tried again. Still nothing. Miraculously, her pistol had jammed. Instinct told me to fire and neutralize the threat, but something stopped me. I hesitated for a second and then decided to take a chance. I rushed the car, hoping I could subdue her before she had a chance to clear the jam and fire. As I opened her door, she threw the pistol on the floorboard and hunched over. I grabbed her left arm and tried to pull her back. She swung at me with her other hand, cutting me across the inside of my left forearm with a razor blade. I grabbed her wrist to control the blade, but my hand slid off. She pulled away from me and grabbed the steering wheel with both hands. I could see that she was cut. I used every extraction technique and pressure point I could think of, but nothing worked. She was psychotic and impervious to pain. Finally, I got a good grip on her left arm. I pulled her from the vehicle and swung her around as hard as I could, driving her headfirst into the rear quarter panel. The impact stunned her, and she buckled. I tried to cuff her, but she continued to resist. She kept screaming and fighting me. I had no choice but to trip her and take her forcefully to the ground. I hollered to one of the bystanders to call for help.

By this time a crowd of onlookers had formed. Tension was growing, and I could tell the crowd was not exactly sympathetic to my cause. They were becoming hostile, and it was understandable. All they could see was a male cop kneeling on a bleeding woman—an attractive, well-dressed bleeding woman. From their perspective, it was simply another case of an overzealous cop using excessive force. They were unaware that minutes earlier she had tried to shoot me. They were unaware that I was cut and bleeding too. I remember feeling really alone. It was like being pinned down in enemy territory with no air support.

To make matters worse, the only available backup unit was two patrol beats away and caught in rush hour traffic.

To make a long story not so long, it was a least thirty minutes after my original call before EMS and backup finally arrived.

Throughout the entire ordeal bystanders stood idly by while I struggled with a psychotic suspect who had just tried to shoot me. Not one person rendered assistance. In fact, a complaint lodged by one of the bystanders resulted in a full-scale internal affairs investigation. That's right. I was investigated for allegedly using excessive force, even though a gun had been drawn on me, and I had been cut while effecting a lawful arrest.

Close Call #5

Case Notes:

The suspect female was eventually committed to a state mental facility after assaulting hospital personnel and ripping sutures from her wrists with a catheter hook.

An on-scene search of her vehicle revealed a box of single edge razor blades, a knife, and a 9mm Luger with a full clip and one round jammed in the chamber.

An internal affairs investigation determined that I had followed protocol and procedure to the letter and used only necessary force to effect the arrest. I was cleared of any wrongdoing and eventually commended for exceptional performance under fire.

CHAPTER 7

STAKEOUT

He will protect his faithful ones, but the
wicked will disappear in darkness. No
one will succeed by strength alone.

—1 Samuel 2:9 (NLT)

"Mark, I just cleared it with your lieutenant. You're riding
with me on a stakeout when you get off tonight. You're
off tomorrow anyway, right?" Famous last words of my
soon-to-be partner for the night.

An hour later, I was in an unmarked 1976 Ford Torino
headed south to a makeshift airfield in the middle of
nowhere. I was wearing my uniform pants and a blue and
white polo shirt. That's right. These spur of the moment
special assignments didn't give you a whole lot of time
to get ready. They were more like, "Throw on a shirt,
Wheeler, and let's go."

My partner was a seasoned narcotics detective who had taken me under his wing and decided to groom me. He informed me that he had credible information that a large shipment of marijuana and cocaine was coming in by air sometime between two and four o'clock in the morning. He told me there would be two or three other units involved in the operation—one each at selected points around the airfield, and one dedicated to a small farmhouse at the end of the so-called runway. We settled in for what appeared to be a long night.

At about four thirty in the morning, my partner, who I will refer to from here on as "IC," said, "I'm going to get some shut eye. Wake me up if anything happens." Minutes later, the other three units conferred and eventually decided to pull off because nothing was happening. IC murmured something to the effect, "Let's just sit tight and see what happens."

Fast forward to about six twenty. It was starting to get light out. IC was still snoozing, and I saw headlights approaching the farmhouse from the north. I rolled my window down to listen. At first, nothing. Then I heard *rat-a-tat-tat. Rat-a-tat-tat-tat. Rat-a-tat-tat.* Dirt started flying in the air all around us. Sparks were coming off the hood of our car. Rounds were ricocheting off the roof. I could see muzzle flashes in the distance. That's right! We were taking automatic weapon fire. It sounded like M16s or Mini-14s on full auto. (Mind you, we had a fully loaded Mini -14 of our own in the trunk.) I drew my Browning Hi-Power 9mm from my shoulder holster and hollered, "Get down!" IC grabbed the radio microphone, turned the PA system on, and hollered, "Police! Hold your fire!" I thought, *Now, that wasn't very smart.* Rat-a-tat-tat. Rat-a-tat-tat-tat. Rounds were still hitting all around us. IC started the engine and threw it into reverse. Now there we were, driving wide open in reverse in an old cornfield, taking automatic weapon fire. The car was struggling to get traction. The ruts and furrows were making it nearly impossible to control the car. We were sliding all over the place. The dust was so thick that we could hardly see around us. Finally we hit a paved surface, the tires chirped, and we were gone.

Close Call #6

Case Notes:

Now, I will spare you the rest of the story. Suffice it to say that I'm just glad I wasn't the detective in charge of this particular operation.

While parts of this account may seem humorous, the fact remains that, for all intents and purposes, we should never have survived that barrage of automatic weapon fire. How all of those rounds missed us remains a mystery to this day. Well, not really. But you know what I mean.

CHAPTER 8

BUSHMASTER
SHOWDOWN

Though I walk in the midst of trouble,
you preserve my life; you stretch out your
hand against the wrath of my enemies,
and your right hand delivers me.

—Psalm 138:7 (ESV)

It was a hazy, overcast day. Temperatures were in the mid-70s. I was on my way to get my patrol car washed and was stopped at the traffic light just a couple of blocks away from the car wash. It was about two o'clock in the afternoon, and I was just sitting there with my window rolled down, listening to Golden Oldies on the FM radio, waiting for the light to change. Right in the middle of "Happy Together" by the Turtles, headquarters aired an alarm activation at the bank just around the corner from me. I started to acknowledge, but I was interrupted by an off-duty lieutenant who said, "We're right here at it, headquarters. We'll check it out." I radioed headquarters, advised them I was close also, and told them that I'd back the lieutenant up. I heard the lieutenant radio, "Ten-six, headquarters. We're out." I was thinking to myself, *They just drove straight in to the parking lot. That's not good.* Before I could even finish the thought, I heard automatic weapon fire. The lieutenant hollered, "ten forty-one, shots fired!" I stomped on it. Smoke poured from the rear wheel wells as my experimental 452 cubic inch engine growled like only a Mopar can. As I approached I could see the lieutenant's solid black unmarked Plymouth Fury in the bank parking lot, not far from the main entrance. I slowed up and pulled over. I could hear rounds being fired. I angled my car for cover. I could see one subject kneeling down at the corner of the bank. He had what looked like a Bushmaster arm pistol with a big clip, and he was opening up on the lieutenant. The lieutenant's car was getting riddled. I couldn't tell if anyone was hit. I was out of range and unable to effectively engage.

Suddenly a four-door sedan pulled through the parking lot and on to the highway, shooting from the car as they turned north. I fell in behind them, but I couldn't get close enough to get a tag number. They began firing at me, so I fell back some more. They were pulling away. About two miles from the bank, they pulled off the road, turned east, and cut straight through the country club golf course. I lost sight of them. By the time I got to the golf course, they were gone. All I could see was tire tracks where they left the road.

To this very day, I don't know how they were able to disappear so quickly.

Once again, I faced automatic weapon fire and survived without a scratch.

Close Call #7

Case Notes:

All of the individuals involved in this robbery were eventually caught and convicted. They were identified either as members or associates of the famed Dawson Gang.

Approximately seven years later (1983), the individual identified (by his own admission) as the one kneeling at the corner of the bank and firing at the lieutenant during the robbery, appeared at a local bank training meeting as a guest speaker. He was brought to the meeting by a local FBI agent who believed that he had been rehabilitated and had enlisted his services in speaking to area banks about bank security (while on parole for bank robbery). My wife, Patty, who was an assistant branch manager, was in attendance at the meeting. At one point during the meeting, he looked directly at her as he commented that when he was robbing banks he wouldn't think twice about killing a police officer in order to escape. That comment has never been forgotten.

He also commented that he had been shot by one of the responding deputies during the robbery cited in this chapter, but he was wearing body armor at the time and wasn't seriously hurt. To my knowledge, this account has never been confirmed.

Not long after this bank security meeting, he was arrested by sheriff's deputies while in possession of a loaded 9mm pistol. He was eventually sentenced to additional time for violating his parole.

Additional note:

Eleven years earlier he had been convicted of manslaughter for shooting a man in the head after brutally beating him during an altercation. Surprisingly, he was sentenced to only four years.

He is now serving a life sentence. He continues to file periodic motions (prisoner petitions) to vacate his sentence.

CHAPTER 9

WHO LET THE DOGS OUT?

---✦---

Blessed is he who has regard for the weak;
the Lord delivers him in times of trouble.
The Lord will protect him and preserve
his life; he will bless him in the land and
not surrender him to the desire of his foes.

—Psalm 41:1-2 (NIV)

It was a cool, slightly overcast weekday afternoon, and I was back home patrolling the Westside. I had recently returned to the Sheriff's Department after serving a six year tour in the air force. About fifteen minutes into the shift, I decided to make a run through City Heights.

City Heights was a massive, federally subsidized, predominantly black housing complex well known for illicit drugs, violence, and a monumental dislike for law enforcement. Over time I had established a rapport with the kids in the complex and often swung by to shoot hoops, throw the football around, and talk "smack," as they would say. The kids affectionately called me "Johnny Mack" (the sheriff's name was Johnny Mack Brown). They were totally enamored with my uniform (gold badge and chevrons, patent leather belt, holster, and boots) and completely fascinated with my PR-24 (police baton made of lexan plastic and aircraft aluminum), which was all dinged up and slightly warped. The older kids would got a kick out of telling the younger ones that it got that way from me crackin' heads (not true, of course). Then they would tell how I was the only one in the department who ever warped one, which *was* true, by the way. So each visit I would give them a quick baton demonstration and a look inside my patrol car. The Remington Model 870, 12-gauge shotgun, mounted vertically just to the right of the steering column, always drew considerable attention. If it had to do with guns, sports, or martial arts, they were totally fascinated.

A few minutes into the visit, I received a call advising of a disturbance at a residence near Paris Mountain, just a few minutes from the complex. Apparently it was carryover from the first shift. There were no details recorded by the off-going dispatcher, so basically I was going in blind on a nondescript disturbance with no immediate backup.

It was customary any time I pulled off on a call for the kids to holler, "Go, Johnny Mack!" This day was no different.

When I arrived at the scene, a white, single-story, frame house at the edge of the woods, I was flagged down by several of the area residents. They told me that someone had broken into the house and was still inside. I advised headquarters that it was a break-in, not a disturbance, and proceeded on foot toward the house. As I approached from the driveway, a stocky, black male wearing an army field jacket bolted from the side door and into the woods behind the house. I advised headquarters that I was in foot pursuit and immediately gave chase. I could hear the dispatcher calling for backup units, but it seemed like the entire platoon was out on calls, and the supervisors weren't on the road yet. After several minutes and approximately a quarter of a mile into the woods, I spotted the suspect in a clearing about fifty yards from the power line right-of-way that ran behind the house. He was about thirty years old, a little over six feet tall, and about 230 to 240 pounds. He was relatively dark-skinned, had a medium length afro, and a patchy beard. In addition to the army field jacket, he was wearing dirty blue jeans and old combat boots. The clearing looked like a campsite. It had a fire pit, a pile of wood, and what appeared to be bedding. As I entered the clearing, I immediately noticed a splitting maul (axe) on top of the woodpile, and several dogs wandering around; one looked like a pit bull mix, one a German shepherd mix, and the others looked like mutts of some sort.

I hollered, "Turn around, place your hands behind your head, and interlace your fingers. Do it now!" As he turned, I could see that he had a large screwdriver in his right hand. I ordered him to drop the screwdriver, and surprisingly he did. As he turned around with his hands behind his head, I hollered again, "Get down on your knees. Do it now!" He just stood there. I ordered again, "Get down on your knees. Do it now!" Again, he just stood there. Concerned about the loose screwdriver, the likelihood he had a knife or gun, and the close proximity of the maul to where he was standing, I decided to cuff him standing and then take him down. I approached with my handcuffs in my right hand, placed my left hand over his interlaced fingers, walked him slightly to the right, pressed him against a tree, and ordered him to spread his legs. I told him he was under arrest and to hold still.

As soon as my handcuff hit his wrist, he went ballistic. He whirled around, hitting me in the face with his elbow and the open handcuff. As I retreated, he charged. Instinctively, I lowered my head and attempted to tackle him, but he was stout and didn't go all the way down. I wrapped my hands around his upper thighs, lifted him off the ground, and attempted a body slam. Right then, I felt something pull in my lower back and an excruciating pain shoot down my left leg. As I weakened under his weight, we hit the ground and rolled. I wound up on my back with him on top. He reached for my service weapon with both hands. Back then we all carried Smith and Wesson Model 10 .38 caliber revolvers with a four-inch bull barrel and +P hollow point loads. I grabbed his hand and my revolver together with both hands and held on. Then I heard my holster unsnap, and I could feel him twisting it, trying to pull it out. As I looked down, I could see he had his one hand completely around the grip and one finger inside the trigger housing. He began squeezing the trigger and trying to pull his other hand free. I could see the cylinder start to rotate. At that point I knew I was in serious trouble. If it discharged in the holster I could be hit in the femoral artery and bleed out before help arrived. If he got it out, well, I was dead either way you looked at it. I held on with everything that was in me. I slipped my thumb under the hammer and tried to keep the cylinder from rotating more. At that point, I remember thinking, *Dying in the line of duty is bad enough, but being shot with your own weapon is worse. I can't let this happen.* Then the adrenaline kicked in. I grabbed his thumb with my left hand and bent it back as hard as I could. He held on for a second or two and then let go. He rolled over and scrambled to his feet. I snapped my holster, drew my PR-24 baton, and stood up. He grabbed the maul from the wood pile and charged me again. As he raised the maul and stepped toward me, I instinctively went for the headshot. As a PR-24 instructor, I knew a headshot was considered deadly force, but he was leaving me no choice. He was clearly trying to kill me. All the while, in the back of my mind, I kept thinking that I could take this guy down without killing him. That's why I never drew my service weapon. As I swung, he dropped the maul and ducked. My baton shaft grazed his shoulder and collarbone area, but his jacket collar deflected and absorbed most of the blow. He seemed stunned. I ordered him to the ground again and stepped toward him with my baton in the cocked position. He hollered, "Get him, boys! Get him!" and ran. Three dogs immediately attacked. I swung to fend them off but lost my grip and dropped my baton. The black shepherd got to me first, sinking his teeth into my right forearm. As he began to shake his head and pull backward, one got me from behind and clamped down on the large tendon behind my knee. The third went for my groin. The pain was excruciating and sickening. I had to choke back the vomit. As I was trying to free my hand, I could hear headquarters on my walkie-talkie repeatedly asking for my location. I couldn't get my hand free to answer. I could hear sirens in the distance and backup units hollering, "Where is he?" When I finally got my right hand free, all I could do was key the mike and holler, "Ten forty-one, Greenville, ten forty-one. Get me some help!" I didn't have time to give a location before one of the dogs attacked again from my left side. I could hear the dispatcher declare 10-33 (emergency traffic). I kicked him twice and reached down to retrieve my baton. When he lunged again, I swung and hit him just behind the ear. He yelped and went down. The others immediately released and ran. The snarling stopped. The woods went silent. I could hear my heart pounding in my ears. Then the welcome sound of sirens yelping in the distance. I remember thinking, *The cavalry is coming. Help is finally on the way.*

To this day, I have no words to describe how I felt when I heard all the radio traffic concentrated on finding me. The concern in the dispatcher's voice and the desperation in each deputy's voice as unit after unit hollered, "Bravo eleven, where are you?" and "Ten twenty, Bravo eleven?" added to the sense of urgency I was feeling. You see—I exited my patrol car and engaged the suspect before I had a chance to report my exact location. All anyone knew was that I was on foot in a wooded area at the base of Paris Mountain. Having been on the responding end many times before, I knew what it was like to hear a fellow officer holler "Ten forty-one" (officer needs help). It was the one ten-code call no one wanted to hear. The one that made your heart skip a beat.

Concerned that the dogs would double back, I drew my weapon. I wasn't sure where I was in relation to the house or on the mountain for that matter, so I stayed in the clearing and waited for backup. My uniform was shredded, and my left leg and back were throbbing. I remember thinking, *Man! That was way too close for comfort!* Physical conditioning and training had saved my life. At least that's what I thought at the time.

Within minutes backup units began arriving. The K-9 tracking unit and Animal Control also responded. It wasn't long before the bloodhounds located the suspect hiding in a crawl space beneath a house about a quarter of a mile from the clearing. I'll never forget the feeling when I heard he was in custody. A part of me wanted to hurt him for what he put me through. Then this incredible sense of grace and compassion swept over me. It would be years before I understood why.

When I got home that night (after several hours in the ER), Patty was sitting on the couch in the dark. My oldest daughter, Becky, was upstairs asleep. The living room was illuminated only by the carriage light outside our front door. I sat down quietly and reflected for a moment. My uniform was torn, and my arms and hands were stained with Betadine scrub from the emergency room. How was I going to tell Patty? How was I going to tell her what had really happened? How was I going to tell her that I had almost been killed? For years I had insulated Patty from the gory details of my job. As I began to speak I could feel the emotion building. My voice began to quiver. Patty started tearing up. I couldn't finish. "Is it worth it?" she asked. I was speechless at first. All I could eventually say was, "I don't know." I must admit this was the first time in my law enforcement career that I truly had doubts.

Once again I had been spared. Once again I had survived a close call.

Close Call #8

Case Notes:

The suspect in this case was eventually convicted of house breaking and grand larceny, resisting arrest, and assault and battery with intent to kill. He was sentenced to ten years confinement with no possibility of parole. The dispatcher who took the original call and whose dereliction had put me in harm's way was terminated after a thorough investigation. Three of the dogs were captured and quarantined. One expired at the scene. Fortunately, none of them ever showed signs of rabies.

CHAPTER 10

ONE FOOT IN THE DOOR

The Lord is my rock, my fortress, and
my savior; my God is my rock, in whom
I find protection. He is my shield, the
power that saves me, and my place of
safety. He is my refuge, my savior, the
one who saves me from violence.

—2 Samuel 22:2-3 (NLT)

For all of you less than avid readers, this chapter is for you.
In fact, this may go down in the annals of book-writing
history as one of the shortest chapters ever written.
Nevertheless, its impact will always loom large in my
heart.

Like any other special operation, this one began with a
briefing. An unusually secretive briefing. I can remember
being called into the office with little explanation. When
I arrived, I was advised that I would be participating in
the execution of a search warrant at a house occupied

by a motorcycle gang known as the Road Jammers. I was aware that several members of our unit had been investigating a motorcycle club for suspected weapons and drug trafficking, but that was about all I knew. I had been deeply involved in an undercover investigation of my own and had been pretty much out of normal circulation for several weeks. Consequently, my knowledge of this particular operation was extremely limited.

During the briefing, I learned that the Road Jammers were believed to be an offshoot or loose affiliate of the Hells Angels. Given the way they were described, they were either serious wannabes or a legitimate prospect charter. Either way, these guys were bad news. That's bad with a capital *B*.

After reviewing a floor plan of the targeted house and a diagram of the surrounding property, we all retired to our vehicles to get suited up. I can remember getting a sick feeling as I removed my ballistic vest and raid jacket from the trunk of my car. As I donned my vest, I thought, *I sure hope this thing can stop a high velocity round.*

I grabbed two extra clips, chambered a round in my Colt Combat Commander (.45 caliber automatic), and away we went.

Fast forward about forty-five minutes.

We were on the grounds. We approached from the rear of the house. We decided to enter via a back door leading to a bedroom. We could see one of the bikers in bed asleep. A Tec-9 (Intratec assault pistol with a 32-round clip) was hanging by a sling from the headboard. JW, the investigator heading the investigation and I were designated the lead entry team. JW was to kick the door down, and I was to enter first. The remainder of the team was to follow. On the count of three, JW kicked the door but missed the frame. His foot penetrated the laminated door completely as it swung partially open. He was caught, fully exposed, with his leg lodged in the door up to his knee as I entered. Now I was exposed without cover and faced with a dilemma. Do I clear the room and protect myself, or cover JW until he can free his leg? I made a spilt second decision and rushed the bed to secure the Tec-9. The sleeping biker, startled by us blasting through the door, rose up and grabbed the Tec-9 as I reached for it. He swung it around and raised it toward my chest. Fortunately, it was caught by the sling. I slapped the muzzle away, pressed my .45 against his temple, and ordered him to let go. Surprisingly, he immediately complied.

Close Call #9

Case Notes:

The operation resulted in the confiscation of numerous weapons, a large cache of ammunition, and several controlled substances.

The Road Jammers MC was formally recognized as a bona fide chapter of the Hells Angels on December 12, 2003. They remain active today.

CHAPTER 11

RAMBO

For the Lord loves the just and will not
forsake his faithful ones. They will be
protected forever, but the offspring of the
wicked will be cutoff.

—Psalm 37:28 (NIV)

Spring 1984

Second Shift Special Operations (Vice & Narcotics)

It was one of those days—long, hot, and boring. We had
spent the first couple of hours of the shift in the basement
of the law enforcement center researching aircraft tail
numbers, organizing intelligence reports, and challenging
each other with trivia questions to ward off the boredom.
About three forty-five in the afternoon, we decided to
take a break and get some fresh air. By "we" I mean me
and our special ops intelligence officer, who was, by the
way, a member of Mensa International (high IQ society)

and a formidable trivia opponent. We started off at the local mall looking at baseball caps and then headed south to an area known for significant drug activity. Just in case you're wondering, baseball caps were a serious part of the special ops regalia, especially for the agents who were hair impaired.

At about four forty-five, the unspeakable happened. Our presupper "where are we going to eat" ritual was interrupted by the sound of three very distinct radio emergency notification tones (or beeps) followed by, "All units. All units. Ten thirty-three traffic. Ten forty-five Bankers Trust, 1927 Augusta Road. Units responding acknowledge."

I couldn't believe it. We had just driven by that bank. And now someone was robbing it.

Within seconds of being given a suspect description and direction of travel, and before we can even turn around, a solo CID unit who happened to be in the area conducting an investigation signed out and advised that he was on foot behind the bank. A couple of minutes passed. We heard gunfire. My heart started pounding. By that time we were about two hundred yards southwest of the bank. I aired, "Shots fired," and jumped out on foot.

Now, here's where it got interesting.

The area behind the bank was an abandoned school compound (for lack of a better description) surrounded by a ten-foot chain-link fence topped with outward angled barbwire. The compound itself was like a big crater loaded with demolition debris and tall grass. It was dotted by several small, algae-covered ponds surrounded by tall reeds. In order to get to where the suspects were last seen and assist the investigator already on foot, I had to scale the chain-link fence and get through the barbwire. To this day, I have no idea how I was able to make it over without tearing myself to shreds. As soon as my feet hit the ground on the other side, I heard the economic crime investigator notify headquarters that he had one suspect in custody. I remember breathing a sigh of relief while at the same time thinking, *Okay, where's the other one?*

For more than an hour I low-crawled through grass and debris trying to locate the second suspect. All the while I was trying to muffle the sound from my walkie-talkie so I wouldn't be detected.

About six o'clock in the evening, the FBI, the local news networks, and the bloodhounds arrived. By now, onlookers were everywhere. Just what we needed— an audience. Can you picture it? I was alone inside a fenced-in compound with an armed bank robber. A bank robber with a shotgun. I was armed with an undercover 2-inch, .38 caliber, 5-shot revolver and no extra rounds. A modest mismatch, wouldn't you say?

Now let me finish painting the picture.

I was crouched down beside a pond covered with a layer of green algae with virtually no available cover or means of concealment. I was completely exposed. The bloodhounds were hot on the trail and heading toward me. They were baying like champs, and the sounds were echoing throughout the compound. Suddenly, the surface algae parted, and the water beside me erupted like Old Faithful at Yellowstone Park. I swung around, and suspect #2 was standing behind me in thigh-deep water with a reed in his mouth. His army fatigues were covered in foul-smelling mud, and algae was dripping from his head. To this day, I don't know who was more surprised, me or him. I raised my pistol to eye level and ordered him to drop his weapon. He hesitated for a second, dropped the shotgun, raised his hands, and pleaded with me not to shoot.

I must admit, this one stayed with me for a while. The thought of a completely concealed, armed suspect barely an arm's length away with the capability of taking me out at any moment was, and still is, incredibly disturbing.

One other thought:

For years I joked about it being the sound of the approaching hounds that compelled this suspect to surrender. Today I know differently.

Close Call #10

Case Notes:

According to bank personnel and witnesses, the pair, clad in green army fatigues and carrying a rifle and shotgun, entered the bank at approximately four forty-five in the afternoon and ordered everybody to the floor. At least one of them jumped the service counter at the teller line. After obtaining money from the cash drawers, he attempted to jump back over the counter but tripped and fell headfirst onto the lobby floor. When he landed he lost his grip on the bag and dumped most of the money on the floor. As the two scrambled to retrieve the scattered bills, one of them apparently dropped the keys to the getaway car, which was parked just outside the door with the motor running and the doors locked. As they exited the bank and realized that neither of them had the keys, they started to argue. After a brief altercation, they split up and fled on foot.

One of the suspects was eventually apprehended by the economic crime investigator who was first on the scene. And of course, you know the rest.

They were both charged by the FBI with bank robbery.

One additional note:

At the time I made this apprehension, I was working undercover on a major cocaine and marijuana importation case. Unaware of my involvement in the undercover operation, the on-scene newspaper photographer snapped a shot of me as I was being assisted by a uniformed deputy. The story was given front-page coverage.

After being given an option by my superiors, I chose to remain on the case, despite the possibility of being made (recognized). Partial results of the operation appear in the photo gallery at the end of the book.

CHAPTER 12

WHICH WAY IS UP?

---◈---

"Because he loves me," says the Lord, "I
will rescue him; I will protect him, for he
acknowledges my name."

—Psalm 91:14 (NIV)

Summer 1984

Sheriff's Department Dive Team

Advanced Open Water Training/Certification

It was a beautiful Saturday morning. There was hardly
a cloud in the sky. If I recall correctly, the lake forecast
called for temperatures in the low eighties, with winds
out of the southwest at about 10 mph. A slight ripple
glistened under the morning sun. It was the final day of
our Advanced Open Water training.

I must admit, I was a little apprehensive—but stoked!
Thanks to a half-price clearance sale, I was sporting a

brand-new O'Neill wetsuit in Marina Blue with Clemson Orange side panels and leg stripes°... and matching gloves. It was a welcome change from the old, battle-worn, hand-me-down dive team suits I had been wearing.

We arrived at the lake about nine in the morning and began to suit up. The Divemasters watched closely as we checked out our gear and went through the predive checklist. After pairing off with our dive partners, we entered the water.

On this particular dive we would be checked out on a variety of skills, including buddy breathing and an unassisted free ascent from thirty meters (one hundred feet).

The dive area was close to a bridge. The descent point was marked by a dive marker buoy. To complete the dive we were to descend (following the anchor rope) to one hundred feet, remove our gear, and ascend at a steady rate, exhaling slowly as we rose to the surface.

When it was finally my turn, I deflated my BC (buoyancy compensator) and started my descent. At about fifteen feet I paused for a couple of seconds to equalize my ears. Normally it would take several attempts, but on this dive they equalized almost immediately. I couldn't believe it. I remember thinking this is a good omen. Just a quick side note: for those of you who have never had the opportunity to dive, there are two things you don't need when you're diving—sinus/ear problems and bowel issues. On this particular occasion I was fortunate enough to be free of both.

I continued my descent.

It was really dark, and I could feel distinct changes in water temperature; warm currents mixed with cold. From my tournament fishing days I knew these transitional layers were called thermoclines. I continued to descend. It seemed like the deeper I got the louder my breathing sounded. I concentrated on keeping my breathing relaxed and steady. Before long a glance at my console confirmed I had hit one hundred feet. I inflated my BC a little and leveled off. As I turned around, I could feel resistance, like something was pulling me back. It was dark, and visibility was poor. I reached back to check my Octopus (spare air system), and it was caught on something. I pulled on the hose, but it was stuck. When I turned to see what it was caught on, I realized that I was entangled in a large ball of monofilament fishing line and tree branches. I tried to untangle myself, but the more I moved the more entangled I became. I dove deeper and tried swimming in different directions, hoping to pull free. Before long, I couldn't tell which way was up. I knew my bubbles would indicate which way was up, but for some reason I couldn't see or feel them. As I struggled with the fishing line my Octopus pulled free, but I still couldn't ascend. I checked my console to see how much air I had. To this day I don't remember what that gauge read. I just knew I had been breathing hard, and my air had to be getting low. I was getting concerned. I was sucking air like crazy. I pulled my dive knife out and tried to cut through the line, but it seemed like for every strand I cut, three more appeared. There were snap swivels and wire leaders and lures caught in the tangle. Submerged tree branches were everywhere. It was a mess. By now it was apparent that I was caught in a pile of brush submerged by crappie fisherman. It was common practice to submerge artificial structures to draw fish. I started feeling light-headed and confused. I was struggling to stay focused and relaxed. Even though I wasn't thinking clearly, I knew exactly what was happening. We had been taught about it in training. I was "narced" (diver slang for suffering the effects of nitrogen narcosis).

For those not familiar with this condition, nitrogen narcosis is simply the result of breathing inert gas under pressure. It produces an altered mental state similar to alcohol intoxication and effects decision making and motor function. Not exactly what you want to experience while tangled up at one hundred feet in dark water. Trust me.

While I was no doubt impaired, I was keenly aware of my location and condition. I knew I was in very deep water and in a really serious predicament. I was feeling very alone. It seemed like the only thing that was keeping me company was the sound of my breathing. I tried desperately to focus and stay relaxed. Then it hit me. A brainstorm. If I inflated my BC, my increased buoyancy would make me ascend. Wow! What a revelation. Why didn't I think of that earlier? I hit my BC with a couple of shots of air, and instantly I began to ascend. The mass of fishing line that entangled me seemed to loosen and fall away. Before long, I was no longer caught.

At this point, you are probably wondering where in the world my dive partner was during all of this. Well, close by, I guess. I later learned that he too had encountered submerged debris and had become somewhat entangled, but not nearly to the extent I had. Due to the depth, limited visibility, and maybe a little inexperience, we had gotten separated. Neither of us was ever aware the other was in trouble. Fortunately, we both surfaced safely. As for how I was suddenly freed from that mass of fishing line and debris, that remains a mystery°... well, not really.

Close Call #11

Case Notes:

The rest of the dives went well, and the remainder of the day was relatively uneventful, with the exception of one case of barotrauma (ruptured ear drum). Everyone completed the training successfully and was awarded their Advanced Open Water Certification.

CHAPTER 13

"GET HIS AFFAIRS IN ORDER"

He will call on me and I will answer him; I will be with him in trouble, I will deliver him and honor him. With long life I will satisfy him and show him my salvation.

—Psalm 91:15–16 (NIV)

Well, here's one more for the less than avid reader. Once again, a short account with life-changing, or should I say, life-altering ramifications. I'll use my journal entries to tell the story.

October 25 through November 1, 2009.

Post-op day eleven.

I've been home for three days recovering from surgery to remove cancer from my colon.

It's about nine o'clock in the evening. I'm feeling really uncomfortable. Something is drastically wrong.

I am experiencing sharp pains in my left side and in my lower back while using the restroom. Patty is assisting me and notices a change in the color of drainage running through one of my JP (Jackson Pratt) drain tubes. It's cloudy and light brown. Patty immediately calls my surgeon. He advises my condition is critical and instructs her to transport me to the emergency room *stat* (that's medical speak for immediately, right now).

After an excruciating ride to the ER, an elephant dose of dilaudid, and a rushed CT scan, the on-call surgical resident determines my anastomosis (that's a medical term for where they reconnected my bowels after removing the cancer) has failed and is now leaking. It's dumping fecal matter into my abdominal cavity. He advises that I am most likely suffering from fecal peritonitis, a potentially fatal condition. Emergency surgery is ordered.

Just shy of nine hours later, I wake up in the ICU.

Patty is the first person I see. The mere sight of her relaxes me.

I ask, "Am I going to make it?"

She replies, "Yes, honey. You're going to be okay."

Later in the day, family members from out of town begin to assemble in my room. Patty's demeanor begins to change drastically. My older sister, a registered nurse of forty-plus years, appears at my bedside. She holds my hand and says, "I'm so sorry, Mark. I wish it was me instead of you." My oldest daughter Becky seems distant and detached. My youngest daughter Megan, the tough one, is showing signs of weakening. My brother-in-law remains stoic in the back of the room.

I'm beginning to sense my condition is critical, far worse than anyone is telling me.

I lift my bedsheets and look down. I have a gaping wound that runs from just below my sternum to my pelvic area. The pain is excruciating, and I am struggling with the effects of the Dilaudid. I'm having trouble telling what is real and what isn't, almost to the point of paranoia. I'm drifting in and out of consciousness. The dreams are frequent and disturbing. I'm losing track of time, and I'm not really sure where I am. I'm feeling so alone. I struggle to keep my eyes open because the dreams are intensifying. They are now demented and macabre. The night seems endless. In my spirit I'm crying out, *Lord Jesus, help me! Please help me!*

Finally, its daylight. I'm not sure what day it is. A group of medical students with laptops and clipboards enter my room. I overhear Patty in the background talking with the nurses about "arrangements." Some time goes by. Then, out of the clear blue, she walks to my bedside and asks, "Mark, where are your military discharge papers? Your DD214?"

Well, at that point, it didn't take a rocket scientist, as they say, to figure out what was going on. Even with all of the painkillers flowing through my veins, I was lucid enough to know that I was in serious trouble. It was apparent that I would soon be in the arms of my Lord and Savior.

It wasn't until weeks later that I learned that immediately following my emergency surgery, my surgeon admitted to Patty that the clean-up procedure had stretched his surgical skills to the max. I also learned that infection issues and the trauma of the surgery had somehow created the potential for multiple organ failure. He suggested that Patty get my affairs in order. In other words, make funeral arrangements and prepare for the worst.

Well, as you can certainly surmise, I survived. Recovery was long and grueling but rich with lessons learned.

Close Call #12

Case Notes:

I would eventually undergo eight more complicated surgical procedures in the five years that followed, one of which left me with a permanent colostomy.

My recovery from each one has been referred to as "nothing short of amazing."

CHAPTER 14

HE'S NOT FINISHED

And I am certain that God, who began
the good work within you, will continue
his work until it is finally finished on the
day when Christ Jesus returns.

—Philippians 1:6 (NLT)

Oh boy! Here we go again. I've been sitting here for almost an hour staring at a blank screen. So many thoughts. So few words. What is the deal?

These were my idle thoughts just before I headed out for an appointment with one of my surgeons this past March. An appointment I had cancelled twice before.

In May 2014, I underwent a complex surgical procedure known as an abdominal wall reconstruction with bilateral component separation. It was performed to repair several massive incisional hernias resulting from eight previous surgeries. As part of my postoperative follow-up plan, I was supposed to meet with one of the two surgeons who had performed the operation every couple of months to make sure everything was still in place, that the biological mesh they had installed was doing its job, and that I was healing properly. This was one of those visits. It was my hope that it would be my last.

Well, my surgeon entered the examination room on that overcast, slightly rainy early spring day, offered the customary handshake, and immediately sat down at the foot of the examining table where I was seated. Unlike my three previous visits, this one was blatantly void of the usual pleasantries. I could tell something was off. "So, Mark. How are you feeling?" I told him that I was feeling good. "Listen, I was just looking at a CT scan you had back in September. Has anyone ever mentioned anything about the spot on your liver?" Spot on my liver? No! They just told me there were no bowel obstructions. I did have a spot on the right side of my liver when I was diagnosed with colon cancer in 2009, but I was told by my surgeon at the time it was a harmless hemangioma. "No, Mark, this is a two-centimeter lesion on the lower left lobe."

As I sat there on the examining table I can remember thinking, *This is not what I was expecting to hear.* Are you kidding me? Setback was the last thing on my mind. This was supposed to be a routine, "Hi! How are you? You look great! See you later" type visit. September? This thing was showing on a CT scan back in September? My mind shifted into hyperdrive. That was almost seven months ago! There's no telling how long that spot has been there. How could they have missed it? *This is not good,* I thought to myself.

Well, after enduring a quick examination of my very sore belly, I retired to the parking lot to process what I had just heard.

Now, I wish I could say this is where I fell to my knees and cried out to God for help, but it wasn't. I simply dialed my oncologist's number as instructed and left a message for his nurse assistant. Then I called Patty to deliver the news.

Although it was never said, both of us knew right then that we were about to embark on yet another incredible journey. We had barely recovered from Patty's battle with breast cancer, and here we were preparing for battle again. *Exhausted* would best describe our condition at the time. We were no doubt battle weary!

About an hour later, I received a call back from my oncologist's nurse. She advised that the doctor had not been aware of the spot on my liver and had ordered an immediate PET/CT scan.

Within a span of approximately three weeks, the PET scan showed my liver spot as "hot," and a subsequent CT-guided needle biopsy confirmed that I was no longer in remission. My cancer had returned.

Diagnosis: Stage IV metastatic liver cancer.

Prognosis: Poor

Little did I know that, as I was about to write the final chapter of this book, I would be given one more close call to chronicle. Maybe the loss of words I alluded to in the beginning of this chapter was more than your garden-variety writer's block. Maybe it was a divinely orchestrated pause as the words were being etched in my heart and placed on my lips, or in this case, the pages of this book.

When news of my cancer returning finally sunk in, I struggled with how I should proceed. Should I write an epilogue? Is God telling me to write another book? How do I incorporate this unexpected event? Is this the beginning of a new work, or the culmination of this current one? Or is it both? And is it actually another close call? After all, couldn't that be a premature determination, given that I haven't survived it yet? Resting firmly in the words of the apostle Paul as he addressed the saints of Philippi from his prison cell: "And I am certain that God, who began the good work within you, will continue his work until it is finally finished on the day when Christ Jesus returns." I decided to continue this chapter in real time—in other words, in the present. I began by sharing my heart publicly with this Facebook post:

> To all my Facebook friends:
>
> Well, the bell has rung. I'm back in the ring (or the cage, for all of you MMA fans).
>
> This afternoon I received confirmation that my cancer has returned. Biopsy has

confirmed what a recent PET scan/CT suggested. I have stage IV metastatic liver cancer.

At present it appears that the tumor is operable.

I will meet with my surgeon in the next few days to confirm the course of action and schedule a date for surgery.

I want each of you to know that I am by no means devastated, depressed, or discouraged by this news. To be so would be contradictory. It would be an inconsistent witness, given the grace and love I have enjoyed throughout my life and the gospel that I have been called to preach. I view this round as one more opportunity to see that God is who He says He is, Jehovah Rapha°… our healer and restorer!

I will remain active on social media as much as I can during my treatment.

Patty and I cherish your friendship and covet your prayers as we look forward to yet another victory.

Grace, peace, and love to you all.

When I received the call from my oncologist confirming the results of my biopsy, he told me that surgical resection appeared possible and asked if I had a surgeon in mind. Not being familiar with the intricacies of liver surgery, I said sure, and named my colorectal surgeon as my first choice. She had performed my last three procedures without complication, and I had implicit faith and trust in her. He said, "Great! I'll call her." Within hours I received a call from her office advising me of my appointment.

Approximately six days later, Patty, my youngest daughter Megan, and I met with my colorectal surgeon. The minute she walked into the examining room you could tell she was deeply disturbed, even though she was trying hard to be upbeat and positive. She had been with me through the toughest of times, and I knew she cared deeply. She advised that she had reviewed my scans and felt without a doubt that the spot was definitely resectable or, in layman's terms, operable. She stated that this particular procedure was a big deal and that she had a highly regarded specialist in mind. She told me that she would contact him before the day was out and set up a surgical consultation. We embraced as we both choked back the tears.

All of us left her office completely deflated. We had expected for her to accept the case and give us a firm date for surgery. Instead we left with no more information than when we arrived. It was apparent that this would be a long, lonely road. The waiting and wondering was killing all of us.

The next thirty-six days would prove to be emotionally agonizing. First, the highly-regarded liver specialist we had been referred to turned us down flat because his practice didn't accept my insurance. Disappointment after disappointment followed, as my insurance was repeatedly rejected by physician groups, hospitals, and cancer treatment facilities. Not only could we not find a qualified surgeon willing to perform my resection, but we couldn't find one who would accept my insurance. Our faith was being tested. Hope was dwindling. Given the knowns about my lesion—that it was more than likely at least a year old; that it was metastatic (colon cancer that had metastasized to my liver), making it stage IV; coupled with symptoms indicative of advanced stage cancer—the survivability models were less than encouraging, giving me weeks at best. The prognosis seemed to be worsening by the day. At times the complacency demonstrated by the insurance community was astonishing and almost unbearable! We were really beginning to wonder.

After more than a month of agonizing disappointment, I received a phone call from a nationally renowned liver transplant surgeon with privileges here in Fort Worth and Dallas. After a brief review of my case, he told me neither his physician group nor the hospital he was affiliated with would accept my insurance but that he would find a way to make it happen. I told him that I was at peace with my diagnosis, and if it was God's plan that my insurance dictate my fate, then so be it. He instructed me to deliver my scans (PET/CT discs) to his assistant here in Fort Worth, and he would call me after reviewing them. I found out later that the plastic surgeon who had recently performed Patty's breast reconstruction had learned of my predicament and he, along with my colorectal surgeon, had contacted this liver specialist on my behalf. Apparently their impassioned pleas made quite a difference.

To make a long story short, after countless phone calls, hours of silence, and unceasing prayer, I finally received a call from the liver specialist's assistant. She advised that the president of the hospital had verified and confirmed acceptance of my insurance and that their transplant team had decided to work in concert to perform the resection free of charge. I was speechless!

On May 19, 2015, the cancer metastasized to my liver was removed from my body along with a portion of my liver. My surgical pathology report could not have been more encouraging.

I am now roughly four weeks post-op and doing remarkably well.

In just a few days, I will begin six months of intense adjuvant chemotherapy to kill any remaining cells and to lower the risk of an additional reoccurrence.

Close Call #13

Case Notes:

My surgery, which was expected to last in excess of four hours, took a little more than two.

My hospital stay lasted only two days.

CHAPTER 15

MAKING SENSE OF IT ALL

The great illusion of leadership is to think
that man can be led out of the desert by
someone who has never been there.

—Henri J. M. Nouwen

The following words (along with those above) will remain
forever etched in my mind and embedded in my heart:

Who can save a child from a burning
house without taking the risk of being
hurt by the flames? Who can listen to a
story of loneliness and despair without
taking the risk of experiencing similar
pains in his own heart and even losing
his precious peace of mind? In short:
"Who can take away suffering without
entering it?"

-Henri J.M. Nouwen

It was roughly twenty-five years ago when I first felt the call to full-time ministry. I was serving as a Eucharistic minister and a fourth grade Sunday school teacher at small Episcopal church in Spartanburg, South Carolina, while working as a division-level executive for a national grocery chain. As a prelude to seminary and prerequisite for Holy Orders (ordination) consideration, I was required to spend a year of reflection and instruction under the tutelage of the parish priest. The first of many assignments was to read and report on a book by Henri J. M. Nouwen entitled *The Wounded Healer.* Little did I know that this little one hundred-page book that spoke about things like woundedness and vulnerability, loneliness and despair, and even accessibility would have such profound impact on my life and ministry. Little did I know that it would eventually bring deeper meaning to the events in my life and answer many times over the ever persistent question, "Why?"

Listen further to what Nouwen says:

> For the minister is called to recognize the suffering of his time in his own heart and make that recognition the starting point of his service. Whether he tries to enter into a dislocated world, relate to a convulsive generation, or speak to a dying man, his service will not be perceived as authentic unless it comes from a heart wounded by the suffering about which he speaks. Thus, nothing can be written about ministry without a deeper understanding

of the ways in which a minister can make his own wounds available as a source of healing.

Okay. You are probably thinking, *What in the world is he talking about? I'm not a minister!* Oh yes you are! We all are. We are all called to minister. Jesus said, "A new commandment I give to you, that you love one another: As I have loved you, so you must love one another. By this all people will know that you are my disciples, if you have love for one another" (John 13:34–35 ESV).

Ministry is a natural by-product of love. When we love someone we have a natural desire to support him or her, to care for him or her, to protect and serve him or her. We "minister" to them. This doesn't require ordination, licensing, or any sort of ministerial credential. Only that we love that person because He (God) first loved us.

How does all of this tie together? Well, if we love people enough to support them, care for them, protect them, and serve them, we should love them enough to be prepared— equipped, if you will.

Now, how does this happen?

Consider this:

In concluding his exhortation, the writer of Hebrews offers the following benediction (blessing):

> Now may the God of Peace, who through
> the blood of the eternal covenant brought

> back from the dead our Lord Jesus, that
> Shepherd of the sheep, *equip* you with
> everything good for doing his will, and
> may he work in us what is pleasing to
> him, through Jesus Christ, to whom be
> glory for ever and ever. Amen. (Heb.
> 13:20–21 NIV, emphasis mine)

As you can see, the writer clearly indicates the same power and spirit that raised Jesus from the grave can, and will, equip us with everything we need to minister to each other in accordance with God's will. Notice he bases his blessing on the eternal covenant. How much stronger can you get than an assurance that has its foundation in the shed blood of the Son of God?

Now take a look at what the apostle Paul says in Ephesians 4:11–12 (NIV):

> So Christ himself gave the apostles, the
> prophets, the evangelists, the pastors and
> teachers to *equip* his people for works of
> service so that the body of Christ may be
> built up. (emphasis mine)

It's very simple. The message is clear. God sees to it that His saints (that's you and me) are prepared and ready to minister to each other. It's up to us to acknowledge His preparation, receive it, and act on it.

Now, in keeping with the honesty and transparency I promised in my introduction, here's where I make my confession. I've always believed God "equips the saints." I've just had a problem acknowledging, receiving, and acting on the preparation He ordained for me. It took me a long time to realize that each significant event, each close call in my life, and each divine appointment was an integral and instrumental step in an ongoing preparation process. As Nouwen so eloquently proposed, I would have to enter suffering in order to take it away, and I would have to visit the desert in order to lead someone out of it. I would have to "bear the wounds" before I could offer them as a source of healing for someone else.

Before I go any further, please hear me. I am not suggesting that everyone has to experience catastrophic events, endure excruciating pain, or survive a series of life-threatening close calls in order to love and effectively minister one to another. God has a perfect plan for each one of us. He has a plan that's uniquely mine, and one that is uniquely yours—a plan that, if acknowledged, received, and acted upon, will bring supernatural healing and joy to your life and ultimately to the lives of countless others.

One other thing before I move on: never let fear dictate your willingness to acknowledge, receive, or act upon what you know in your "knower" that God is directing you to do. Rest comfortably in the assurance He gives us in Isaiah 43:2 (NLT):

> When you go through deep waters, I will
> be with you. When you go through rivers
> of difficulty, you will not drown. When
> you walk through the fire of oppression,

you will not be burned up; the flames will
not consume you.

Remember: going through the rivers of difficulty will either cause you to drown or force you to grow stronger and better equipped. If you choose to operate on your own strength, you are more likely to drown. If you acknowledge God's plan and invite Him to go with you, He will protect you, and you will be fruitful.

Okay. Let's wrap up some loose ends.

If you remember—in my introduction I proposed that the events in our lives are not random isolated occurrences but rather divinely orchestrated providential experiences that prepare us for a much greater purpose. I went on to say that it was my belief that God allowed the events in my life, specifically the close calls, to shape me and prepare me for the call He had given me. Now, I am sure many of you are wondering how in the world I arrived at this conclusion. You're probably also wondering what *divinely orchestrated* and *providential* means. Well, in the way of explanation, and for the sake of brevity and clarity, I offer the following extracts from Wayne Grudem's *Systematic Theology: An Introduction to Biblical Doctrine*, regarding God's providence. I trust his treatment of this subject will answer these questions.

God's Providence

Preservation:

God keeps all created things existing and maintaining the properties with which he created them.

Concurrence:

God cooperates with created things in every action, directing their distinctive properties to cause them to act as they do.

Government:

God has a purpose in all that he does in the world and he providentially governs or directs all things in order that they accomplish his purposes.

We read in the Psalms, "His kingdom rules over all" (Ps. 103:19). Moreover, "he does according to his will in the host of heaven and among the inhabitants of the earth; and none can stay his hand or say to him, "What are you doing?" (Dan. 4:35). Paul affirms that "from him and through him and to him are all things" (Rom. 11:36), and that "God has put all things in subjection under his feet" (1 Cor. 15:27). God is the one who "accomplishes *all things* according to the counsel of his will" (Eph. 1:11), so that ultimately "at the name of Jesus" every knee will bow "in heaven and on earth and under the earth, and every tongue confess that Jesus Christ is Lord, to the glory of God the Father" (Phil. 2:10–11). It is because Paul knows that God is sovereign over all and works his purposes in every event that happens that he can declare that "God causes all things to work together for good to those who love God, to those who are called according to his purpose" (Rom. 8:28 NASB).

Note: In Ephesians 1:11, the word translated "accomplishes" (energeo in the Greek) indicates that God "works" or "brings about" *all things* according to his own will. No event in creation falls outside of his providence.

The Decrees of God

The decrees of God are defined as *the eternal plans of God whereby, before creation of the world, he determined to bring about everything that happen*s. This doctrine is similar to the doctrine of providence, but here we are thinking about God's decisions *before the world was created*, rather than his providential actions in time. His

providential actions are the outworking
of the eternal decrees he made long ago.

Wayne Grudem is a research professor of Bible and
Theology at Phoenix Seminary in Phoenix, Arizona. He
previously taught for twenty years at Trinity Evangelical
Divinity School in Deerfield, Illinois. He holds a BA
in Economics from Harvard University, an MDiv and
DD from Westminster Theological Seminary, and a
PhD in New Testament Studies from the University of
Cambridge.

CHAPTER 16

FINAL THOUGHTS

It's a beautiful Tuesday morning, and I am sitting here in the infusion center receiving my chemo treatment. Patty is sitting faithfully beside me. I'm praying, reflecting, and wondering. Where do I begin? How do I finish?

Throughout this reoccurrence ordeal and during the last five to six weeks in particular, I have received several cards and handwritten notes (or missives as she would refer to them) from a dear high school friend. Yes, in the age of social media, e-mail, and text messages, handwritten correspondence still exists. And how refreshing it is.

Contained in one of her recent cards, along with expressions of love and words of encouragement, was this prayer (commonly referred to as the Prayer of Saint Francis):

> Lord, make me an instrument of your peace. Where there is hatred, let me sow love; where there is injury, pardon;

where there is doubt, faith; where there
is despair, hope; where there is darkness,
light; where there is sadness, joy.

O Divine Master, grant that I may not so
much seek to be consoled as to console,
to be understood as to understand; to be
loved as to love; for it is in the giving that
we receive; it is in the pardoning that we
are pardoned; it is in the dying that we are
born again to eternal life.

Now, I could very easily finish this book right here with
an exhaustive review, a laundry list of takeaways, and a
study guide. But I won't. I would rather leave you with
this. Embodied in this prayer is the essence of why we
exist: to be instruments of His peace and to bring glory
to His name. Each one of us is given within our lifetime
every opportunity to be equipped and instrumental in
the kingdom of God. Whether or not we acknowledge
and accept this assignment is clearly a matter of choice.
Simply put, I have chosen to acknowledge and accept.
How about you?

BENEDICTION

The Lord bless you and keep you; the Lord make His face shine upon you and be gracious to you; the Lord turn his face toward you and give you peace.

—Numbers 6:24–26 (NIV)

Shalom!

EPILOGUE

If you recall, way back in chapter 1, I used the story of the Israelites crossing the Jordan River and their twelve-stone monument (found in the fourth chapter of Joshua) to lay a foundation for my recollections and to propose a parallel with the twelve close call events that ultimately shaped my life and ministry. Little did I know that in the course of telling my story, I would be given an opportunity to acknowledge and experience a thirteenth-stone event: one more close call.

I'm offering this brief epilogue for one reason. And that is to share with you, after considerable introspection and prayer, what I glean from this unexpected continuation of my story.

My conclusion is simple. The message is abundantly clear. Neither you nor I are finished until God is.

The driveway where it all began.

Rookie photo

Bravo Platoon (1975)

Military decorations

Special Operations—cocaine/vehicle seizure

My first college graduation after entering
the air force (Patty at my side).

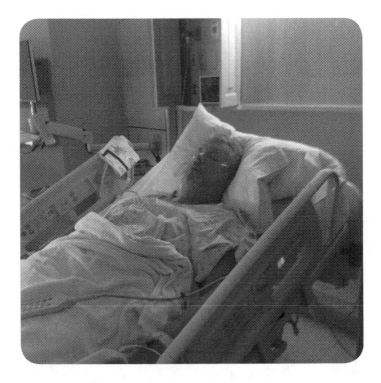

In recovery after my liver resection.

Walking the halls with Patty hours
after my liver resection.

BIBLIOGRAPHY

Grudem, Wayne. *Systematic Theology*. England: Inter-Varsity Press/Zondervan, 1994, p. 315–333.

Maas, Peter. *Serpico: The Cop Who Defied the System*. New York, NY: The Viking Press, 1973, p. 49, 268.

Nouwen, Henri J. M. *The Wounded Healer*. New York, NY: Doubleday, 1990, p. xvi, 72.

Printed in the United States
By Bookmasters